SISTAOLOGY

When the Holy Spirit Breathes on Black Women's
Stories

By
Rochelle Haggins

Sistaology
When the Holy Spirit Breathes on Black Women's Stories

Published by Women's Empowerment Network
ISBN: 979-8-218-73837-2

Printed in the United States of America
First Edition, 2025

This is a work of nonfiction. Any resemblance to actual events or individuals, living or dead, is intentional and rooted in the lived experiences and testimonies of Black women.

For permissions or inquiries, contact:
Women's Empowerment Network LLC
Email: womensempowermentnetworkllc@gmail.com
Website: www.womensempowermentnetwork.net

Cover and interior design by Rochelle Haggins.

Dedication

To the women who taught me to stretch, to sit in silence, to break without shame, and to rise anyway.

To the mothers, the daughters, the elders, the sisters, and the sacred friends.

To those who carried oil when no one noticed.

To those who preached with their living and prayed with their weeping.

To every Black woman who survived the fire and still sings.

This is for you.
You are the theology.
You are the movement.
You are the miracle.

Acknowledgments

To the One who breathes life into dry bones—Holy Spirit, thank You for speaking through every scar and singing over every storm.

To my beloved husband, Rev. Josiah Haggins—thank you for standing with me, praying for me, and holding space for me to become. Your faithfulness has been a quiet fire beside mine.

To my children—Josiah II, Joy, and Julius—you are the most remarkable story I will ever tell. Watching you rise reminds me to rise too.

To my spiritual mothers, mentors, and seminary circle, thank you for pouring into me when I had nothing left to give. You reminded me that the oil never runs dry when it comes from heaven.

To every woman who said "yes" to being interviewed, to being vulnerable, to showing up for the Women's Empowerment Coffee Break—your voice echoes in these pages.

To my readers, thank you for opening your hearts to this sacred journey. I pray these words hold your wounds, honor your wisdom, and stir your flame.

And to every sista who feels unseen or unheard—this book is not just for you.
It is because of you.

Table of Contents

Introduction

This Book Is Liturgy

This book is not just meant to be read —
It is meant to be **felt**.
Prayed through.
Wrestled with.
Spoken aloud.
Torn open and poured out like oil.

This is not a manual — it is a movement.
Not just theology, but testimony with rhythm.
This is Sistaology — sacred, sound, and Spirit-led.
You will not find traditional chapters here.
You will encounter **movements** —
Shifts, groans, waves, and winds of the Holy Spirit.
Each movement carries its own sound.
Its own testimony.
Its own outpouring.

You may find yourself weeping in one,
worshipping in another,
and rising in the next.

Every movement is liturgy.

Every page is praise.

Every section is a sanctuary.

My story calls — and yours will answer.

My tears will fall on these pages — but so will your freedom.

Let this book become your **upper room**.

Let it become your altar, your sanctuary, your healing bench.

Let it read like **testimony**. Let it rise like a **prayer**.

Let it breathe like **liturgy**.

Because when we talk about *liturgy* here, we are talking about the sacred order of a service. The way God moves through the room. From call to worship, to confession, to word, to sending. Except here, the service is our lives. And every testimony is a sermon. Every tear is an offering. Every yes is the benediction.

This is not a textbook. This is a holy gathering. A space where our stretch becomes strength. Where our silence becomes sound. Where our breath becomes bold.

So come as you are — Faithful or frustrated. Tired or on fire. Sure or searching. Because the Spirit is already here.

And She is about to move. Here are the movements the Spirit will lead us through:

Movement One: The Stretch

When the yes hurts
Obedience that costs. The weight of the call.
This movement explores what it means to say yes to God,
even when it hurts. You will hear the groan of surrender and
the whisper of purpose rising through the pain.

Movement Two: The Silence

When God goes quiet
Stillness, waiting, sacred frustration.
Here we wait, not in stillness alone, but in sacred frustration.
You will meet the God who listens to groans, answers
through people, and invites you to write even when the next
step is hidden.

Movement Three: The Breath

When the Spirit whispers
Holy Spirit moments — dreams, visions, revelations.
Here is the wind. The fire. The unexplainable leading of the

Spirit. This movement gathers every divine interruption and Spirit-led moment that shifted the course of your journey.

Movement Four: The Story

When you finally speak

Testimony time. Sacred storytelling as theology.

Here, we testify.

We remember.

We tell the truth about what we've lived — not to stay there, but to give God glory through it.

Movement Five: The Break

When the community fails

Loneliness, disappointment, sisterhood truths.

This is where we name the wounds that came not from enemies, but from within our own circles.

But this is also where we heal, where truth is balm, where disappointment makes way for divine restoration.

Movement Six: The Rise

When voice becomes power

Finding your rhythm, your authority, your oil.

This movement is where resurrection begins.

Where you speak with confidence.

Where you no longer shrink to fit in — because your Spirit
has found its rhythm.

Movement Seven: The Fire

When others catch the flame

Legacy. Multiplication. Anointing. The bridge.
This is where your obedience becomes someone else's
deliverance. Where what you carried becomes a mantle.
Where your story becomes a movement.

Let every movement **minister** to a different part of you.
You do not have to read them in order — follow the wind.
Follow the ache. Follow the **Spirit**.
And come back to them as needed.

And now, before we begin, this introduction will serve as our
opening prayer.

Holy Spirit, come.

Before we turn a page, turn our hearts.
Before we read a word, ready our souls.
We are here, tired, but here.
Wounded, but still breathing.
Pressed, but still present.

So, Spirit of the Living God —
Fall fresh on every woman who holds this book.

Let her feel seen in these pages.
Let her feel heard in these lines.
Let her feel held in this moment.
Let this not read like another book —
Let it move like worship.

Let it sound like testimony.
Let it unfold like sacred liturgy.
Let these words not just be mine,
but yours — breathed, broken, and burning with truth.
May every chapter become an altar.
Every reflection become a release.
Every story become a song of freedom.
This is not just a book.
This is a holy gathering.
We invite You into this space, Holy Spirit.
We will not rush past You.
We will not speak over You.
We will not silence the groan or the glory.
We give You the tears.
We give You the joy.

We give You the questions.

We give You our "yes" — even when it shakes.

For the sistas who stayed.

For the ones who are stretching.

For the ones who are waiting.

For the ones who are weary, but not done.

Come, Holy Spirit.

Make these pages burn with Your presence.

And it is so, Amen.

Prologue: When the Spirit Stirs

This is not just a book. It is a breath. A bridge. A baptism in oil. These pages were born from whispers in long nights of wrestling, from stretches that almost tore me in two—but never took me out. And I believe, if you are holding this book in your hands, then you, too, have survived some kind of stretch. You, too, have sat in silence that felt like abandonment, waited in rooms that never called your name, and risen anyway—with trembling knees and holy fire in your eyes.

This is a theology that was not taught in a classroom but lived in a prayer closet. It was carried in the womb of Black women who had to become both altar and offering, both question and answer.

You are not reading this alone. You are reading this with your grandmother's prayers wrapped around your back. With your sister's strength in your bones. With the breath of the Holy Spirit hovering over every page, waiting for you to inhale what has been prepared just for you.

So come open.

Come honest.

Come tired, if you must—but come with expectation.

Because God is still moving in the language of Black women and still speaking through our scars, oiling our ashes, and igniting something eternal in those who thought they had nothing left to give.

You are not behind.

You are not too late.

You are not broken beyond repair.

You are the miracle this world did not see coming.

So may the fire of Sistaology fall upon you now—
Not to consume you, But to commission you. Not to scorch you, But to sanctify the stretch you are in. Let the Spirit stir. Let the movement begin.

Movement One: The Stretch

When The Yes Hurts

Obedience never comes without a pull.

"Blessed is she who has believed that the Lord would fulfill His promises to her." — Luke 1:45

I did not expect obedience to feel like this. Nobody tells you that saying yes to God might stretch you until your skin feels thin and your prayers feel hoarse. But that is what a yes does — it pulls you until you become unrecognizable to people who only knew you before the oil.

I said yes to God.

To seminary.

To ministry.

To dreams I once buried and dared not name. And when I said yes, life did not get easier. It got heavier.

Let me tell you how I knew I was in the stretch: I was a full-time student, a full-time wife, a full-time mother, a full-time preacher, a full-time women's ministry leader — and I still had to remember to eat. I was cooking dinners and writing papers in the same breath. I was writing sermons with tears running down my face and holding my babies while asking God to hold me.

Every time I thought I could rest, something else cried out for me. Laundry. A deadline. A child. A congregation. My own body.

I did not feel holy. I felt tired.

The night before I preached my senior sermon, I could not stop crying. I had been silent all morning. My body showed up in class, but my spirit did not.

"God, how am I supposed to preach like this?" I whispered, broken.

And the Holy Spirit said, "Preach anyhow."

So I did. With tears still dried on my skin and strength I did not know I had, I opened my mouth. And when I tell you The Holy Spirit moved — oh, She moved.

That is the stretch. When your strength runs out, but the Spirit steps in.

It did not stop there. Two weeks later, I was sitting on the edge of my bed, surrounded by silence. I had no idea what came next. The heavens were quiet. I had prayed for direction for months, and still, nothing.

But the Spirit was not absent. She was waiting.

And then, like a breath on the back of my neck, She whispered: "Write the book."

That was the beginning of this. Not just a project. Not just a calling. But a birthing.

I had already named it in a journal assignment: Sistaology.

And I realized then — God had been preparing me to speak from my stretch. Not from my arrival. Not from my ease. But from the pull.

Here is what I need you to hear, sis: The stretch does not mean you are failing.
It means you are growing.
God is not punishing you — God is preparing something in you that comfort could never produce.

You feel unseen, but God is shaping you in silence.
You feel tired, but you are being taught how to lean, not carry. You feel like the rubber band is about to snap — but you are being prepared to hold more than you thought you could.

You are not being punished. You are being prepared.
For fire. For testimony. For glory.

And it hurts — I know. I cried, too. I begged God for release, too. I said, "God, just tell me what's next" — and all I heard was, "Be still."

But stillness is not silence. It is strategy.

That stretch? It is sacred. It is not here to break you — it is here to birth you.

I reached a place where I had nothing left to pour.

The assignments were due.

The children needed dinner.

The church needed leadership.

My husband needed partnership.

And my soul?

It just needed rest

I did not hide it.

When I was not okay, it showed. I was not the kind of woman who smiled to survive. If you looked at me, you knew I was struggling.

But I still kept saying yes. Some days with a whisper. Some days with tears. But still, I said yes.

The Woman Who Bled

The stretch that changed everything. If I had to name the biblical woman who mirrors my soul, It would be **her** —
The one who bled. The one who went unnoticed by everyone But *recognized by God.*

Twelve years. Twelve long, aching, faith-testing years. She did not just bleed — **She stretched.**

You can find her story in Mark 5:25–34. A woman unnamed, yet unforgettable.

Imagine the profound voyage of faith, healing, and restoration. Woven into every movement of her body. Imagine her breath, labored.

Her body was frail.

Her hope was trembling.

Jesus was on His way to heal a synagogue leader's daughter — but this woman? This **unnamed**, **unclean**, **unseen** woman stretched herself into His story.

She had suffered at the hands of doctors. She had spent all she had. She had endured being cast aside, whispers of "unclean," glances that looked away.

And still — **She reached.** She pressed through a crowd. That had never bled like she bled. Who had never been isolated like she had. Who had never carried shame in their bodies the way she did.

She stretched beyond what was permitted, beyond what was polite, beyond what was proper.

Because when desperation dances with faith, protocols are no longer the priority — **healing is.**

I imagine her not just crawling, but *moving with intention*. Each step a sermon. Each breath a prayer.

She became a living choreography of pain and hope, echoing every sista who ever felt unseen but still reached for wholeness anyway.

That is my stretch. That is *Sistaology*.

I know what it means to be surrounded and still feel alone. To be pressed on every side — by expectations, by responsibility, by exhaustion — and still find the strength to reach.

I have been her. Bleeding and stretching. Wounded and hoping. Tired and still moving.

Her story was not written just to inspire — it was written to *mirror* the sacred stretch within each of us. She did not have a name in the text, because her name could be **mine**. It could be **yours**.

She symbolizes the Black woman still bleeding behind the smile. Still showing up while silently breaking down. Still pressing her way through the crowd — not for applause, not for recognition, just for a touch.

And here is the miracle: **Jesus stopped for her.** He turned toward her. He called her *daughter*. He didn't just heal her body — He restored her identity.

Mark 5:34 He said to her, "Daughter, your faith has made you well; go in peace, and be healed of your disease."

The Stretch will do that. It will pull things out of you that you thought were dead. It will cause Jesus to stop in the middle of His journey just to speak life over you.

You may feel hidden now. But your stretch is about to get God's attention.

You may feel like your story does not matter. But your reach is about to shift the narrative. So stretch, Sis.

Stretch beyond the pain. Stretch past the silence. Stretch even if your hands shake. Because if you can just touch Him — even if only the hem — everything can change.

Mark 5:28 *for she said, "If I but touch his clothes, I will be made well."*

Holy Anger and Honest Questions

Let me be honest. I got mad at God.

Not the kind of anger that turns you away from Him — but the kind that comes when you are standing in front of the door God told you to knock on, and still, it will not open. I said, "God, I love You — but I am tired of the quiet." Not the kind of silence that soothes — but the kind that stings. The kind that makes you question every yes you have given.

I wanted answers. I wanted relief. I wanted just one prayer to get a yes without a test. I remember pacing my room, feeling like my prayers were bouncing off the ceiling. I said, "I gave up everything to follow You. I left comfort. I left familiarity. And you are quiet? Why would you stir up this calling in me — and then surround it with confusion?"

I cried hard that night. I groaned from a place deeper than words. I asked God, "Did I miss You? Did I hear wrong? Because I feel like I'm running toward a promise that keeps disappearing in the fog."

But even in the midst of my frustration, I refused to feign peace that I did not feel. Worship is not always a song. Sometimes, it is a sigh, a groan, a truth spoken through trembling lips. I was not about to slap a Scripture over my soul to seem strong.

Because I needed God to hear me — all of me. The holy and the hurting. The faithful and the frustrated.

And here is what I learned: The Holy Spirit is not intimidated by your honesty. She is not offended by your questions. She meets you in the messy places.

I felt Her presence not when I was quoting Scriptures out loud, but when I whispered, "God, I do not understand You right now. But I still believe You are here."

That moment — that *raw* moment — was worship too. It is a sigh. A tear. A truth you are brave enough to say out loud.

So if you are angry, say it. If you are confused, name it. The Spirit does not need you to be polished. She needs you to be present.

And trust me — She will show up. Right there. In the holy wreckage of your honesty.

The Sistas That Showed Up

I thank God for the ones who did not try to fix me — they just sat with me. No formulas. No sermons. No pressure to smile. Just presence. That was enough.

Sometimes healing does not come in the form of advice — it comes through *ears*. Open. Willing. Nonjudgmental ears. God sent me sisters who did not require me to be strong when I clearly was not. They did not quote Scripture at me as a shield against my pain. They simply held space — holy space — for me to be.

One friend encouraged me and said, "I do not have the answers. I just wanted to remind you that I get it." It was as if the Holy Spirit was speaking through her words, reminding me, "You do not have to be everything for everyone right now. Let God be everything for you." Those words were on repeat like it was worship music. Because it *was*.

It was worship in the form of sisterhood. Worship in the form of someone showing up. I remember one conversation where I did not even have the words to explain what I was going through. I started a sentence and could not finish it.

I just sighed. And she said, "You do not have to finish. I feel you. And I'm standing with you."

That moment broke something open in me. Not because she had the answers — but because she was willing to hold the questions with me.

They did not make the time I had with them about them. They simply listened to my frustrations. That was the Holy Spirit — using my story to set me free and organizing ears to hear what my soul could not say out loud.

That is what Sistaology means to me. It is not about fixing each other. It is about *feeling* with each other.
It is about recognizing that sometimes your presence is the prayer. Sometimes your quietness is the balm.
Sometimes just showing up is how you help someone survive the stretch.

So if you have ever been the one who listened — thank you. And if you are longing for that kind of sisterhood — do not give up. The Holy Spirit is still sending women who will sit in the dark with you until the light comes back on.

The Stretch and the Spirit

Here is what the stretch taught me about the Spirit: She is not just a comforter — She is a coach, a counselor, a midwife, a fire-starter. She was not standing at a distance watching me struggle.

She was in the middle of the labor with me, whispering, "Push."

The stretch taught me that the Holy Spirit does not always calm the chaos. Sometimes, She breathes through it. She does not always rescue you from the fire. Sometimes, She teaches you how to walk through it without being consumed.

I thought the stretching was punishment. But it was actually permission. Permission to grow. Permission to go deeper. Permission to see just how much power God had already placed inside of me.

Because let us tell the truth: comfort never reveals your capacity. It is the stretch that exposes your strength. It is the stretch that activates your faith. It is the stretch that tells you — "You can carry this. Not because you are strong, but because I am with you."

When everything in me wanted to collapse, the Holy Spirit spoke to my spirit and said, **"You are being made into something new. This is not the end — it is the transformation."**

I started to understand why oil has to be crushed out of olives. Why wine must be pressed out of grapes. Why new life must be pushed through pain. This stretch was not here to destroy me. It was designed to birth something I could not carry in my old strength. It was creating new lungs in me to breathe deeper, praise louder, trust harder.

Sometimes the stretch does not come with an explanation. It just comes with grace. And if you can stay in the process — if you can hold on through the pulling and the pressing — glory will meet you on the other side.

That is what happened with *Sistaology*. I did not plan it. I was too tired to produce it. But in the middle of the most overwhelming season of my life, the Spirit whispered, "Birth it."

And I did. Not because I felt ready, but because I felt *led*. So let me speak this over you, sis: If you are in a stretching season, do not shrink. Lean into it. There is oil in this tension. There is glory in this groaning. There is purpose in this pull.

God is not just stretching you for endurance — God is stretching you for expansion. Because what is coming *through* you is bigger than what is pressing *against* you.

Spiritual Surrender

At some point in the stretch, my prayers changed. I stopped asking God to hurry up. I stopped begging God to lift the weight. I started praying for **purpose**, not relief.

Because I realized — this stretch was not random. It was sacred.

I used to pray, "Lord, fix it." But now I found myself whispering, "Lord, keep me." Keep me from giving up. Keep me from collapsing under doubt. Keep me grounded when everything around me feels uncertain.

I fasted like my future depended on it. I pressed in with prayers that did not sound pretty — but were soaked in desperation. I cried out in my heavenly language when words failed me. Because I knew something had to break — and I was not sure if it would be the circumstance or my own fear.

There were days I laid prostrate, face to the floor, with nothing left to say but "Help." And even that one word was a full-body surrender. I surrendered my timeline. My image. My need to understand it all.

I realized that surrender is not weakness — it is worship. It is not the end of your power — it is the beginning of God's. It is saying, "Lord, I trust You even when I do not trace You." It is letting the Spirit lead, even when you cannot see more than the next step.

That is the posture that gave birth to Sistaology. Not certainty. Not clarity. But surrender.

And sis, I want you to know — it is okay if you are not strong every day. It is okay if your faith looks like showing up with tears. It is okay if your praise sounds like a whisper.

Because the Spirit is not looking for performance. She is looking for honesty. And every time you open your mouth and say, "God, I am still here," Heaven rejoices — because you have not let go. The stretch did not break me. It built me.

And when the stretch pushed you beyond your limits, the Spirit did not rush you. She whispered, "Now rest. Now listen. Now breathe."

God's movement is not always loud. In the silence, we are reminded of 1 Kings 19:12—God was not in the wind or the fire, but in the still small voice. In Sistaology, silence is not emptiness; it is a holy strategy.

From the ache of obedience, we slip into the hush of waiting. The Spirit does not rush. She listens in the stillness.

Reflection Prompt

Take a moment and ask the Holy Spirit:

Where am I being stretched?

And what are You birthing through the pressure?

Write it. Cry it. Testify it.

Let it break you open so the oil can flow.

Movement Two: The Silence
When God Goes Quiet
Stillness. Waiting. Sacred Frustration.

"Be still, and know that I am God." — Psalm 46:10

No one likes to go through this part. The part where the heavens close their mouth. The part where you pray until your throat dries — and still, God says nothing.

No signs.

No burning bush.

No lightning bolt.

Just silence. And I am not talking about the kind of silence that feels peaceful. I am talking about the kind of silence that feels like abandonment.

You ever sit in your room, Bible in hand, tears falling down your cheek, and whisper — **"God, are You still there?"** I have. More than once.

I remember one night in particular — I sat in the house office with the lights off. The only glow came from the streetlight bleeding through the window. And I said with all the honesty I had left: **"God, if this is obedience, why does it feel like abandonment?"**

I had said yes.

I had surrendered.

I had obeyed. And still, I could not hear a thing. That is the silence that cuts. The kind that makes you question everything you thought you heard. The kind that makes you wonder if you missed a turn, dropped the assignment, or disappointed Heaven. Stillness is not passivity — sometimes it is prophetic.

Sometimes, God goes quiet not to forsake you, but to develop you. Because when the noise dies down, you hear the deep things. The buried things. The scared parts of you that you try to drown out with productivity.

It is in the silence where God shows you the real you. I used to hate the quiet. Now I recognize it as sacred.

Because it was in that silence that the Spirit gave me the next step. It did not come with a trumpet. It came with a whisper. And even that whisper had to fight through the noise of my doubt.

Months before, I had written a paper on Sistaology. It was raw, Spirit-led, and personal. I had no idea what it would become. But my professor saw it. She looked at me and said, **"You need to keep developing this. There's something here."**

At the time, I nodded — unsure. I filed the comment away. Because I was still trying to finish the semester, raise a family, and survive seminary.

But then, the next semester, I registered to take that professor again for "Idea of Pentecost" — that same professor assigned a final paper, asking me to bring this theology to life. She asked me to perfect what I had already begun.

That was confirmation. That was God breaking the silence through a vessel. So, I wrote it. Not just to submit an assignment, but to steward the sound I heard in silence. To honor the whisper. To say to the Spirit, "I'm listening. Even when it hurts. Even when it's quiet."

That paper became the foundation of what you are holding in your hands right now. *This* is what the silence was preparing me for.

The silence taught me how to *wait with worship.* To *linger* without answers. To *trust* even when direction feels delayed.

Stillness became my sanctuary. And I realized: waiting on God is not passive. It is spiritual warfare. It is a declaration that I will not move until God moves with me.

So to every woman waiting in the quiet — You are not being punished. You are being positioned. And when the Word comes, it will be worth the wait.

Waiting

So yes, I know what it means to wait — and not just in my calling, but in my body. I waited until marriage.

And sis, let me tell you — that kind of waiting will test everything in you. Your patience. Your identity. Your belief that obedience is still beautiful.

There were so many moments where I wondered if it was worth it. People laughed. Some rolled their eyes. Some said, "Nobody's doing that anymore." But I held my ground.

Not out of pride. Not out of shame. But because I knew what God had whispered to me as a teenager: **"You are mine. Set apart. Covered."**

I remember writing my senior yearbook quote: **"Everybody's not doing it."** That was my banner. My quiet declaration that I would not follow the crowd — even if I walked alone.

And yes, the waiting was lonely. Yes, there were days I questioned it. Yes, there were temptations and tears. But I stayed.

And not because I was perfect. But because God kept me when I did not want to be kept. He gave me a way of escape. God covered me in silence. And in that stillness, God was writing a bigger story — one of healing, identity, and power.

People think waiting is weak. But waiting is warfare. It is saying, "I will not let my body move until the Spirit says move." It is saying, "I trust God's plan more than my pressure."

And when that waiting turned into a wedding — when that prayer turned into a promise — when that silence turned into celebration — I knew the waiting was holy.

So now when I wait in other areas, I remember what God did when I waited in *that* area. And I say, "Do it again, Lord. Even in the quiet."

Because if God met me in the waiting once, God will do it again.

When Stillness Feels Like a Sentence

I used to believe the silence meant I had failed. That God's quiet meant I had failed somewhere — missed a cue, taken a wrong turn, disqualified myself. I would replay every decision. Every delay. Every "yes" I had spoken. And still, there was no answer.

Now I know it was forming me. **The silence was not personal. It was purposeful.** Sometimes, silence is how God detoxes your spirit from the noise. From the need for people's applause. From the false belief that productivity equals favor. From the pressure to perform when God just wants presence. Stillness taught me to stop striving and just sit. It taught me to stop running and just rest.

Silent Seasons are Sacred Soil

Waiting feels unproductive — but it is actually deeply prophetic. The most fruitful things grow in hidden places. Seeds do not sprout in the spotlight. They take root in the dark. In the dirt. In the quiet

And that is what silence is: Sacred soil. It is where roots grow deep before the fruit is ever seen. It is where trust is tested. Where pride is broken. Where humility takes shape.

I used to hate that part. The part of ministry, motherhood, and purpose where nothing seemed to be growing. But now I see it. God was growing *me*.

Because what I was asking for could not rest on shallow soil. God had to dig deep. Break ground. Clear stones. And then — plant something holy.

So if you are in a silent season — bless the soil. Something sacred is being sown. 1 Kings 19:11–13 reminds us that God was not in the wind, the earthquake, or the fire — but in the whisper.

11 He said, "Go out and stand on the mountain before the Lord, for the Lord is about to pass by." Now there was a great wind, so strong that it was splitting mountains and breaking rocks in pieces before the Lord, but the Lord was not in the wind; and after the wind an earthquake, but

*the Lord was not in the earthquake; **12** and after the earthquake a fire, but the Lord was not in the fire; and after the fire a sound of sheer silence. **13** When Elijah heard it, he wrapped his face in his mantle and went out and stood at the entrance of the cave. Then there came a voice to him that said, "What are you doing here, Elijah?"*

Sometimes God does not shake the mountain.

Sometimes, Holy Spirit just breathes.

God's Delay Is Not God's Denial

There were moments I wanted to quit.

Moments when the only thing keeping me from walking away was the memory of what God had said. Not what God was saying — because I could not hear God. But what God had **already** spoken.

I had to cling to past prophecies like a lifeline. To reread journal entries. To pull out sticky notes from my prayer board and whisper, **"Lord, I'm still holding on."**

And the enemy would whisper, "If God really called you, it would not be this hard." But I have learned — **Delay does not mean denial.**

And silence does not cancel the promise. It sanctifies the promise. It matures it. It gives it weight.

So when the fulfillment comes, you do not just celebrate it. You carry it with reverence. Because you know what it cost. You know what it took to hold on when nothing made sense. You know how it feels to worship with a cracked voice and a confused heart.

And yet — you stayed

You kept showing up.

You kept praying.

You kept believing.

Sis, that kind of faith is holy.

Holy Frustration Has a Purpose

Let us talk about it, sis —

that tension you feel when you know God is real, but you still feel forgotten. It is the frustration of having faith but feeling like the promise is playing hide-and-seek.

You believe.

You obey.

You tithe.

You pray.

And still — nothing moves.

And if you are like me, you start to ask: **"God, what am I doing wrong?"** But sometimes the answer is: **Nothing.**

You are not doing anything wrong. You are in the silence. And that silence feels like *holy frustration.*

It is not frustration born of rebellion — It is the ache of waiting while still worshiping. The cry of "God, I trust You, but this hurts."

That is a sacred place.

Because it is in *that* place where the oil of testimony is crushed out of you. Where the fire of your call is kindled. Where your voice becomes sharp with truth.

Holy frustration is proof you still care. That your spirit is still alive. That you are still reaching for Heaven when Earth gives no answers.

And here is what I want you to hear: **God honors that kind of honesty.** You do not have to hide your groans. The Spirit translates them.

You do not have to fake joy. The Spirit births it. You do not have to pretend to be okay. The Spirit covers you in the meantime.

So if you are frustrated —you are not failing. You are being formed. And that formation will not be wasted.

From Stillness to Sound: The Spirit Speaks

I will never forget the moment the Holy Spirit broke the silence.

It did not come with fireworks. It came with clarity. Gentle. Strong. Sure.

"Write the book."

Three simple words that carried the weight of glory. Three words that unlocked everything I had been praying for. Three words that reminded me: **God had never left. God had just been waiting.**

Waiting for my heart to be still. Waiting for the distractions to settle. Waiting for me to trust God — even in the fog.

I grabbed my laptop.

And I wrote.

I poured.

I prayed.

I obeyed.

And Sistaology came alive — not from the mountaintop, but from the silence. From the stillness. From the surrender. From the holy frustration that turned into fire.

The silence was not God's absence. It was sacred preparation. The silence did not break you—it blessed you. And in that sacred stillness, the Spirit began to breathe again.

The breath of God (ruach) was the first gift given to humankind in Genesis 2:7. When we lose our breath, we do not lose our worth. The Holy Spirit is the midwife who brings breath back to weary lungs.

Even silence inhales. And then—exhale. The Spirit breathes, interrupting what we thought was the end.

Reflection Prompt:

Take a deep breath, sis.

Now ask yourself — and ask God:

"What am I carrying in silence that I have not yet cried out loud?"

"What am I angry about that I have been too afraid to name?"

"Can I trust that even this frustration is holy ground?"

Let the tears fall if they need to.

Write what aches.

Write what you are tired of waiting for.

Write what you are still believing for — even if your faith feels thin.

Then ask the Holy Spirit:

"What are You refining in me through this frustration?"

Sit with Her.

Listen.

Let the oil come from your groan.

Movement Three: The Breath

When the Spirit Whispers

Dreams. Visions. Holy Instructions. Revelation.

Then the Lord God formed man from the dust...and breathed into his nostrils the breath of life." —
Genesis 2:7

Not every move of God comes with thunder.

Sometimes, the Spirit speaks in symbols, in dreams, in a breath.

In the kind of whisper that you do not hear with your ears, but with your soul.

This is the movement of breath.

Of divine nudges.

Of the gentle wind that stirs your spirit in the night and says, "Go this way."

There was a night when I had a dream that I have never forgotten.

I was 18.

In the dream, I was in a car — but it had two steering wheels. I was sitting on the passenger's side, trying to drive.

When I tried to turn right, the car went left. When I tried to turn left, the car went right.

Frustrated, I got out and moved to the driver's side, determined to take control. But the moment I tried to start the car — it would not move.

It was completely off.

And I woke up.

Immediately, the Spirit revealed the meaning:

I had been trying to drive from the wrong place.

I thought I was not in control, so I shifted.

But the whole time, God was showing me that even when things do not go my way, I am still in the right place — if I let God steer.

That dream was a breath from Heaven.

A soft but strong reminder that God's direction does not always look like my plan.

When I woke up, I could not shake it.
That car haunted me—in the holy kind of way.

And slowly I understood:

That dream was not about transportation. It was about transformation. God was showing me that my instructions were already in my hands. That obedience was the ignition. And movement would not happen until I stopped waiting for clarity and started trusting the call. That one dream became the blueprint for the bigger one.

What I saw with my eyes closed became what I pursued with my eyes wide open. So now—when I talk about dreams, I am talking about those quiet, sacred visitations that become the loudest push of your life.

This movement is for every sista who has had a dream and doubted it. Every woman who heard something in her spirit but thought, "Maybe that was just me."

Every soul who woke up with a vision, a word, an instruction — and questioned if it was holy.

It was.

It is.

The Holy Spirit is still breathing.

Still revealing.

Still hovering like She did in Genesis — over the chaos, over the unknown, over your womb of becoming.

Here is where we honor the quiet power.

Here is where we name the God of whispers, the Divine Midwife, the Breath of truth. This is the movement that does not shout. It exhales.

And in that breath is instruction, restoration, and direction. You may have been waiting for thunder — but God might be speaking through the breeze.

You may have been looking for lightning — but Heaven may be writing on your dreams.

Let this be your permission to believe again in what you saw. To remember what God showed you in the dark. To revisit the journal entry. To pick up the promise. Because what the Spirit breathes on — lives.

There are some dreams you never forget — not because they were dramatic, but because something in your soul recognized them as divine.

When The Dream Speaks Again

That car dream? It never left me. I still feel the tension in my hands from steering in the wrong seat. But even that tension became revelation —God was steering. I just had to trust the wind.

And yet, that moment became power in my spirit. It became the framework for how I live, how I listen, and how I lead. Because the truth is — I was never meant to drive.

I was meant to discern the movement of the car and trust where God was taking me. I was meant to surrender control before I even reached for it. That is what breath does.

It brings revelation that becomes regulation — not rules, but rhythm. The Spirit began teaching me something else through that dream: when you follow the whisper, provision follows the movement.

When you surrender your grip, power returns to your soul. After I woke up from that dream, I stopped chasing my own path and started asking God for God's plan.

After pursuing a career in culinary arts, God stopped right in my tracks. That is when I heard it, "Do social work."

And I obeyed — not because I had the full picture, but because I trusted the breath that gave the word. I left the kitchen, not knowing that I was stepping into my calling. And when I stepped on Troy University's campus, a different kind of fire was lit.

That is where I birthed a movement. That is where Women's Empowerment first stirred in my belly. The whisper of God became the work of my hands.

And here is what I have learned since then: Sometimes the Spirit repeats Herself — because She is waiting for you to believe Her. God does not mind confirming what was already breathed.

God will send reminders. Echoes. Patterns.

God will speak through people. Through pain.

Through professors.

Through that same journal you forgot you wrote in.

The whisper will come again.

And when it does — move.

Sometimes we wait for loud, when God is whispering through the quiet. Sometimes we wait for confirmation. But what we really need is courage.

And yes — sometimes the whisper sounds too big for you.

Too holy.

Too weighty.

You will want to shrink it down to your comfort zone.

But let me say this clearly, sis:

If it scared you and still stirred you — that was God. If it felt holy and heavy and still yours — that was the breath. You do not need a title to trust the breath. You do not need a platform to walk in power.

All you need is a yes. And when you give it — watch how God writes your story with wind. And the whisper got louder — not in volume, but in *urgency*. That is what breath does. It may start soft, but if you listen, it builds.

The breath becomes a breeze.

The breeze becomes a wind.

And the wind becomes your witness.

I have also been the breath for others. I have spoken words I did not plan to say — truths that had to come from God, because there was no way I could know that kind of pain on my own. I was nervous. I questioned myself.

But then I remembered: This is not about me. This is the Spirit choosing to speak.

So I opened my mouth. I said what was dropped into my spirit. And every single time — Tears. Breakthrough. A knowing. One person said, "Only God could have told you that." And they were right.

So I say to you, beloved: Do not dismiss what came to you in a whisper. Do not downplay your dreams. Do not ignore the breath.

Your imagination is not too wild — It is prophetic. Your vision is not too far — It is divine. Your instruction is not too strange —It is *holy*. Let God speak through symbols. Let God move through nudges. Let God write on your spirit in ways only you can understand.

Because this is not just a story. This is a map. This is a wind tunnel of revelation. This is the Spirit speaking in dreams and visions and firelight.

You are not crazy. You are *called*. You are not reaching. You are *receiving*. Let the whisper rise. Let the Spirit move through you. Let your next yes be written in the wind.

When God Shows You Something

I have only had one vision in my life. But that one vision was enough to change the way I listen to God forever.

It was not during a fast.

It was not in a prayer closet.

It was not in the middle of a storm or struggle.

It was in church — during the closing song.
Nothing dramatic. Just the regular rhythm of Sunday.
And then suddenly, like a screen opened in my soul,
I saw her.

A young woman, standing nearby — but in the vision, she
was not in the pew. She was smiling, glowing — doing a
pregnancy photoshoot.

The image was so clear it startled me. I knew her. I knew
she had no children. And yet, what I saw could not be denied.

I was not imagining. I was beholding. It came fast. Like a
download from Heaven. I did not have time to reason or
question or doubt. The Spirit said it — and I believed it. And
I told her. There was no fear in it. No trembling. Just a holy
urgency to speak what I saw before the moment passed.

I do not say that lightly. Because there have been times in
my life when I have hesitated. Times when I have said, "God,
is this You?" Times when I have paused, searching for clarity,
asking, "Is this just my mind? Or is this a word for someone
else?"

But in this moment, the clarity came with peace. And months later — just like I saw — she was pregnant. Carrying the very promise I had seen in the Spirit.

I still remember how it felt to watch that vision become reality. It was not pride. It was not "I told you so." It was reverence. Wonder. Worship.

God had trusted me with a glimpse. And it came to pass. Let me say this to you, sis: Visions are not about control or credit. They are about trust. God gives them not because we are worthy — but because we are willing to carry what others cannot yet see.

Sometimes the vision will be for you. Other times, it will be for someone else. But always — always — it will be for God's glory.

And here is what the Spirit taught me about discernment: Timing and intent. Not every revelation needs to be spoken right away. Not every vision is for public declaration. But when the Spirit nudges, when the instruction comes — obey. That is how I walk with God now. I ask, "Is this for me to hold or to release? Is this about ego or about edification?"

And if the Holy Spirit keeps pressing, I release it.

Even when I feel unsure.

Even when it costs me comfort.

Because I have learned that God speaks in images. In symbols. In flashes of holy insight that drop into your spirit and do not leave until you make room for them.

It reminds me of Hagar — the God who sees, seeing her in the wilderness. God did not only speak with words — God revealed a promise. That is what visions are: a glimpse of what God is growing,
even when it is not yet visible.

So, if you have ever seen something and wondered, "Could this be God?" Let me tell you — God still gives visions. God still speaks through the unseen. And if God is showing it to you, it is because there is purpose in your sight.

Do not rush to explain it.

Do not rush to prove it.

Just honor it.

Because God does not just speak through thunder. Sometimes God shows up in a closing song. A quiet moment. A whispered image that lingers longer than logic can't explain.

That is the breath.

That is the vision.

Let it settle in your bones.

Let it guide your next move.

Let it remind you that if God shows it —
God will bring it to pass.

Holy Instruction: When the Spirit Says Move

Some instructions are not shouted. They do not come with
lightning or loud signs. They come as breath. They come as a
nudge. They come when you are tired, unsure, and out of
plans — and God whispers, "Move."

I was not looking for a ministry. I was not looking to build
a movement. I just wanted to be faithful.

So I started with six women.

No pulpit.

No platform.

Just a gathering of hearts — open, bruised, and hungry for
God. We prayed. We studied. We told the truth.

And week by week, Women's Empowerment grew.

That yes — that one yes — became the soil for something
sacred. A ministry. A mantle. A mission. I am still walking in
it today. But God did not stop there. The next instruction
came unexpectedly. "Josiah is your husband."

It was not just about love.

It was about legacy. It was about being yoked with
someone who carried vision. Someone who would cover me

when I cried, pray for me when I doubted, and say yes to the Spirit with me.

We married.

We served the church.

We raised our family. And we followed the Spirit wherever She led. Then came another whisper: "Start uploading videos for Women's Empowerment."

By then, I had not touched the ministry in years. Life had taken over — Wife. Mother. Graduate student. Tired. But after a Daniel's Fast, God asked me plainly, **"What are you waiting on?"**

So I picked up my phone. No lights. No cameras. Just Spirit. I recorded what I had. And Heaven breathed on it.

I posted on Facebook. Then Instagram. Then YouTube. And the breath of God moved. Women started reaching out. Testimonies started coming in. And I realized — God was doing it again. This was not performance. This was purpose.

Every time I followed God's instruction, it cost me something —

My control.

My plans.

My comfort.

But every time, it carried me into something greater than I imagined.

Then came Princeton Theological Seminary.

I had no plans of applying.

But God kept placing it in front of me.

Everywhere I turned — there it was. A post. A picture. A nudge. So I prayed. "If I see one more Princeton post before I go to bed, I will apply."

I saw it.

I applied.

I got in.

And my husband said, "If you get accepted, we will move."

So we did. We sold our home. Left our familiar life in Alabama. Packed up our children, our dreams, and our fears — And moved to New Jersey.

No job.

No church.

No guaranteed provision.

Just instruction — and a promise that God would meet us there. I started seminary before my husband even had an appointment. Those early months were uncertain.

Uncomfortable.

Unsettling.

But still — the Spirit moved.

He transferred to the First Episcopal District. And in November, he was appointed a church. God made a way. God made a way. God made a way.

Through every tear.

Through every paper. Through every lonely night and early morning class — The Spirit sustained us. That was not just schooling. That was a sacred assignment.

And now, here I am —Seminary behind me. Ministry before me. And my last instruction right here in your hands.

God is not done breathing. And the same Spirit that whispered to me is whispering to you. You do not need every detail. You just need to follow the wind.

The instruction may not make sense. The timing may feel terrible. The road may not be paved. But if it is God — then the breath will carry you.

Revelation

Some revelations do not come in prayer closets. Some come through pressure. Through the silence before the "yes," through the tears in your pillowcase, through the moment you look in the mirror and say, "This is bigger than me — but somehow, I was still made for this."

I remember standing in front of a congregation, preaching a tag team sermon from the story of Esther, and realizing as the words left my lips — this was not just a sermon. It was a revelation.

Esther was not born with a robe or a title. She was born with favor and fire. And it took the stretch of a situation — the shaking of her world — for her to realize what she carried.

That was me too.

I had plans. I had peace — or at least, I thought I did. But God allowed everything around me to shift. Not because I was being punished, but because I was being positioned. The title of that sermon was, "Do not be mad — I was made for this." And even as I said it, I felt the Spirit breathe on the inside of me, "This is the revelation I have been waiting to show you."

Revelation is not just about seeing visions. Sometimes it is about seeing *yourself* the way God sees you. Even when the world still sees your wounds. Esther had to stand up in a moment she never expected. She did not choose the crown — the crown was placed because she had the courage to carry it.

That day, I realized: Revelation comes when you stop shrinking. When you stop disqualifying yourself.

When you stop waiting for the pain to pass and instead say, "If I perish, I perish — but I will go."

The Holy Spirit whispered through that sermon: You were made for such a time as this — not once you feel ready. Not once they see your worth. But now. While the pressure is present.

That word did not just minister to the congregation — it changed me. Because revelation is not just what God shows you. It is what God *activates* in you.

The anointing on Esther's life was not announced by trumpet. It was revealed in a moment of choice. And so is yours.

You may be waiting on confirmation — but what if the confirmation is in the call? What if the sign you are looking for *is you still standing*?

God does not always send thunder and lightning. Sometimes God sends you. To stand. To speak. To survive.

Sis, I want you to sit with this: You are not just carrying a story — you are carrying revelation. And every time you choose to obey, every time you choose to speak, every time you show up in rooms you were never expected to enter, the Spirit is whispering again,

"You were made for this."

The breath did not just speak—it sent me.

With new breath in your body, it is time to speak. Not the story they told about you—but the truth you were born to carry.

Revelation 12:11 says, "They overcame by the blood of the Lamb and the word of their testimony." Testimony is theology embodied. Your story is sacred text—written in your walk, your wounds, and your witness.

With breath comes boldness. And with boldness, the stories rise. Your voice remembers what silence tried to bury.

Reflection Prompt:

Take a moment to slow down.

Breathe in deeply.

And ask yourself:

When was the last time you knew it was God — not your thoughts, not your fears, not your plans — but the Spirit whispering something holy into your life?

Maybe it came as a dream.

Maybe it arrived as a whisper.

Maybe it sat heavy in your spirit like a word you could not shake. Maybe it was an instruction, a vision, a sentence in your journal, a name that would not leave your heart.

Reflect on these:

What dream, vision, or word have I doubted because it felt too big for someone like me?

What am I being invited to breathe life into?

Now write it.

Pray over it.

Speak it into the atmosphere.

Let the Spirit hover. Let the breath move. Let the whisper rise.

Movement Four: The Story

When You Finally Speak

Testimony time. Sacred storytelling as theology.

"And they overcame him by the blood of the Lamb and by the word of their testimony, and they did not love their lives to the death." — **Revelation 12:11**

I have always been a storyteller. **And let me be clear—** I am not talking about the kind of story people tell to escape the truth. Not the kind of story that covers, conceals, or distorts. Not fiction. Not lies.

I am talking about the kind of story that tells the truth even when it trembles. The kind that does not shy away from the hard parts, the holy parts, the healing parts.
The kind of story that testifies—openly, honestly, and without apology.

These are not just stories. **They are testimonies.** They are offerings of truth laid at the feet of God, where even the broken parts become sacred.

Story is not just what happened. It is what God revealed in the happening. It is theology wrapped in lived experience.

When I tell my story, I am not just recalling—I am remembering. I am putting broken pieces back together in the presence of the Holy Spirit. This is sacred work. Because when a Black woman testifies, when she dares to speak truth in a world that thrives on her silence, **that is theology.**

Not the kind buried in footnotes or confined to pulpits, but the kind that breathes. The kind that heals. The kind that knows God not just through doctrine, but through deliverance.

"They overcame by the blood of the Lamb and by the word of their testimony..." That Scripture is not symbolic—it is strategy. It tells us that testimony is not just storytelling. It is warfare. It is survival. It is the first step to thriving.

And deeper still— Story is a study. It is a lived study of who God is, how God moves, how the Spirit shows up in the middle of chaos, and how Jesus keeps resurrecting what we thought was dead.

Sacred storytelling is theology in motion. It is exegesis from the underside. It is the unfolding revelation of God through our breath, our memory, our pain, and our praise.

This is sacred storytelling.

It is theology in the key of survival. Theology in the rhythm of healing. Theology in the tone of truth.

Our stories are not side notes to Scripture.
They are echoes of it. Just like the Psalms, the Prophets, the Gospels— our voices carry the same Spirit. And when we speak, we do not just remember what happened. We reveal who God has been. And we keep learning who God still is— through us.

Because I learned a long time ago—if you do not tell your story, your silence will start speaking for you. Not the kind who needs a microphone, but the kind who learned early on that holding it in can break you open in the wrong places. Because I am the redeemed—and the Bible says, *"Let the redeemed of the Lord say so." (Psalm 107:2)*

My story. My yes. My song. And I will not let shame steal my voice. That silence, when swallowed too long, will find a way to scream—through your body, your choices, your outbursts. I learned the hard way: if you do not speak your truth, your truth will speak *for* you.

And sometimes? It will speak in the form of an explosion. I have had too many of those. Too many moments where the words I held back came out sideways, sharp, messy, untimed. Until one day, the Spirit said, "Enough." It did not come with thunder. It came with a memory. A conversation. A 17-year-old girl sitting in her childhood bedroom, staring at her best friend, and finally letting the truth come out.

I can still see it. That old house—100 years of stories soaked into the wood. Ceilings that stretched higher than our teenage dreams. And me, with my fists full of unspoken things. We argued. Over something I cannot even remember. But what I do remember is this: Shanate looked me in the eye and said, "Why didn't you say something when it happened? I can't fix what I do not know."

That was it. That was the moment.

The Spirit spoke through her, and I heard it like a thunderclap: **"Speak. Not to destroy, but to be understood. Speak to be received."**

That conversation became sacred. It was my first altar of release. I opened my mouth even when it felt uncomfortable to me and others.

And from then on, I could not go back to silence.

But telling the truth? It costs.

Not every part of my story was for public consumption. Some pieces are too raw, too precious. You do not just throw your pearls in the wind. But when the Spirit says share it, I do. Even when I know they might twist it. Even when I know they might run and tell it to ears that were never meant to hear. I have done that—spilled my heart to the wrong ones. I've seen the smirks behind my back and the fake smiles to my face. I've heard the gossip echo down pews and group chats. And yet—I was still free. Because I told it.

Because what was once a weight became wind in my lungs. Because my voice, once shackled by shame, found its key. Telling the truth cost me my perfect identity. But I flew above it. And something broke open.

Once I told it, I realized—it was the best decision I ever made. I felt lighter. I cannot always see the ripple effect. But I believe someone out there was touched. Maybe she could not say it aloud. Maybe she never sent the message. But I believe she heard something in my words that stirred the Spirit in her.

And God? God was already waiting on the other side of my obedience. **God met me in the story by showing me grace.** In some moments, the healing was immediate. In others, it was slow—grief stretched out over time. The deeper the wound, the longer the healing. But healing came. And the breath of God never left.

And now, sis— Let me turn the mirror to you. Because this is not just my testimony. This is our altar. Our echo. Our collective remembering.

You may not feel ready, but sis—your story still lives.

So pause for a moment. Get still. Breathe. And let the Spirit ask you gently: **What has silence cost you, sis?** What part of you did you lock away just to survive?

Where did you lose your voice?

Was it in the classroom, the church, the kitchen, the courtroom?

In that relationship? In that job? In that grief? What story have you buried that is begging to breathe again? The one that makes your hands tremble, your eyes water, your heart say, "Not this one. Not yet."

But what if *this one* is the one that will set somebody free? What if your obedience becomes another woman's breakthrough? You are not alone. You are not crazy. You are not too late. You are not too much. You are a part of this story.

Let the room become your release. Let the page become your pulpit. Let your tears become the ink. Because the Spirit is still saying: **"Speak. Testify. Rise."**

Because Sistaology is not just theory. It is not just theology—it is *testimony*. It is the sound of a Black woman setting herself free by speaking what hurt her and what healed her.

Let me talk to my younger self—and maybe yours too:

Baby girl, this world will try to shut you up.
They will call you dramatic, angry, too much. They will honor your survival but shame your scars. They will say "strong Black woman" and never ask what broke you.

But Sistaology says: You are not just part of the story—you *are* the story. And God is still writing through you.

This is not quiet work. This is fire. This is testimony in motion. This is theology in the key of "I've been through too much not to speak."

This is the kitchen table. The hair salon. The hospital room. The protest line. The church pew. The prayer closet.

This is where the Holy Spirit walks barefoot and says, "This ground right here? This is holy." And it is. Because we are still carrying too much. Still bleeding in secret. Still shrinking to fit spaces not built for our fullness.

But hear me—

No more hiding.

No more shrinking.

No more waiting for permission to speak.

Sistaology is the sound of Black women standing tall and saying: **"I have something to say—and the Holy Spirit backs me when I speak."** We need this. Because survival is not the finish line. We are not here just to endure.

We are here to *flourish*.

Sistaology tells the truth about the pain— but it also tells the truth about the *power*. Yes, we cried. Yes, we bent. Yes, we nearly gave up. But we are still here.

And that too—**that too is theology.**

Recently, I began renovating a house— and I thought I was ready. I had the vision. I did the research. I was excited.

But once the work began, I realized: **Renovation is not pretty.** It is messy. It is slow. It is expensive. And sometimes, it reveals more problems than you expected.

I made mistakes.

I got tired.

I wanted to quit.

But when I stepped back and looked at what had been restored, I saw something holy. The house was not perfect— but it was better than it had ever been. **So was I.**

That house became a metaphor for my life—
A life that has endured misdirection, disappointment, and detours. But when the Spirit starts restoring you, You do not just look different— **You are transformed.**

And oh—the Spirit.

She is not just in the pulpit.

She is in the hush between two Black women who see each other's scars. She is in the "me too" that slips through tears. She is in the labor pains, the lonely days, the "God, I cannot do this anymore." She whispers what no one else can. She breathes new life over what looked like nothing.

Sistaology is what happens when we let Her breathe. And sis—if your voice still trembles, if your truth still feels too raw, if your story still hides behind the tears that dare not to roll down your checks— **it is okay.**

The Spirit is not in a rush. She is patient. She is kind. She is near. She will wait with you in the silence. She will rock you in the ache. She will hold your words until you are ready to release them.

And when you do speak—whether it is a whisper, a sigh, or a full shout— She will be there to catch every word and carry it straight to the heart of God.

You are not less holy because you are still healing.

You are not less powerful because you are still quiet.

Your silence is not shame—it is sacred ground preparing to bloom. **Speak. Testify. Rise.**

Your story matters. It was never too small. It was never too late. And it was never too much for God.

You are a living, breathing Sistaologist. Let the fire in your bones testify. Let the breath of God pour through you.

And when you speak? May the whole room catch wind of the Spirit and say, **"Surely, God was in this place."** Sometimes your story leads to a breaking. Not because you are weak, but because the vessel must make room for new wine.

Psalm 34:18 reminds us, "The Lord is close to the brokenhearted." In *Sistaology*, the break is not the end—it is where the anointing begins to leak out.

Sometimes our stories fracture in the telling. Sometimes community breaks instead of holding. But even in breaking, there is balm.

Reflection Prompt: Let the Story Speak

Take a moment and reflect:

What story have you been carrying in silence?

Where in your life did your voice begin to shrink?

What would it sound like if you let that story breathe?

Write about a moment when you felt the nudge to speak but held back. Then write again—this time as if the Holy Spirit was sitting next to you, saying, **"I am right here. Say it. All of it."**

Let your story speak.

It does not have to be polished.

It does not have to be perfect.

It just has to be *true*.

Because your story is not just survival—it is sacred.

It is theology in motion.

And when you tell it, God shows up in the telling.

Movement Five: The Break

When Community Fails

Loneliness, disappointment, sisterhood truths.

"He heals the brokenhearted and binds up their wounds." — Psalm 147:3

This one is hard to write. Because this is where the pain came from places I called home. From people I sat beside. From those I prayed for. Showed up for. Believed in.

The break did not come from a stranger. It came from silence. From those I had poured into when they had nothing to give. It came when I looked around and the ones I thought would be there—were not.

I was pregnant with our second baby. It was a smooth pregnancy—until 34 weeks. I woke up in unbearable pain. Ran to the bathroom. Blood. So much blood.

I was rushed an hour away to the nearest hospital with a delivery unit. I prayed the entire ride. And when we got there—there was no heartbeat.

No one dreams of planning a funeral when they were just preparing a nursery. I was devastated. And I will be honest— many showed up. I felt love. Support. Prayer.
But even in the kindness, I could feel who was missing.

The ones who said I was their sister. The ones I never thought I would grieve without. It broke something in me. Because what do you do when you are drowning in grief, and the people you thought would carry you— are nowhere to be found?

I tried not to focus on who did not come. But their silence screamed. I wanted to be stronger. I wanted to be grateful. But all I could think was: "Where were they?"

It broke the day I realized maybe... **I did not matter as much to those who mattered to me.** I was not asking for a miracle. I was hoping for presence. I did not need them to fix it.
I needed them to stay.

In the loss of my child, some showed up and wrapped me in love. But even then, I still felt the ache of those I thought would have been there—and were not.

Still, that was not the only break.

There were other moments, other seasons, where no death had occurred—only disappointment. No tragedy—only silence. Moments when I was celebrating a milestone or navigating hardship, and those closest to me simply did not show up.

That is where it stung the most. I spoke my disappointment. Gently. I prayed. But something in me closed. My trust? Fragile. My openness? Guarded.

After it happened, I found myself... Trying to pray through a heartbreak I could not name out loud. Because what cut the deepest was not their absence in one moment. It was the pattern. The echo of too many seasons where I had shown up for people who could not—or would not—do the same for me.

And it made me question not my worth— but the nature of love I had accepted for too long. Still, I looked inward too. There were seasons when I could not be the strong friend either.

Times when I was barely holding myself together. And I know I missed moments that mattered to others. But I have come to learn— when people are hurting, your reasons sound like noise. They do not want to hear what you were going through. They want to feel seen. So did I.

And when the break happens — whether intentional or not— sometimes it cannot be undone. You try to show up differently, but they have already stepped away. They do not owe you a return. They are protecting their peace.

But what about my pain? **And then there was the loneliness.** Not just a moment— but a thread that has quietly run through my life.

It was not because people were cruel. Most times, it was not even intentional. They had their own burdens. Their own families. Their own grief. And I understood that. Truly.

But I have a family too. I have responsibilities too. And still—I made space. I rearranged. I showed up. I made it work. So when others could not—or did not— a quiet ache settled in.

It was not the absence that hurt most. It was the way their support did not quite land where I needed it. They checked in. They circled back.

But it was not the kind of presence my soul was aching for. Not the kind that says, *"I will sit in this with you—not fix it, not rush it, just be here."*

And that question haunted me: Am I asking for more than people can give? But the Spirit whispered back: "No, daughter. You are not asking for too much. You are just learning what others are able—or unable—to give."

That was the ache: Not rejection— but reality. So I carried it. Not with bitterness, but with a quiet kind of grief. The kind that builds over time. And still, the Spirit met me in it.

Not with answers. But with presence. In the long pause. In the held breath. In the silence after disappointment. She was there.

Not one ache was wasted. Not one tear went unnoticed. Even here—especially here—God saw me. There is no closure—only space. Only me and the Holy Spirit. Only memories that once held joy and now carry a sharp edge.

And even still... the Spirit is faithful. God met me in the break by holding the ache and giving me room to grieve what I never thought I would lose. Reminding me that even when the circle gets smaller—Her presence gets stronger.

I forgave. I am still healing. But I no longer carry the illusion that love always returns the way it was given.

I am still healing, but now I know Romans 8:28 is more than a verse. It is a lifeline. It is God turning even this—into something I can rise from.

To the one who's hurting in silence: I want you to know you are not too much. You are not too sensitive. You are not imagining things.

You are carrying real hurt from people who should have been safe. And that pain deserves a voice. You are not crazy. You are not bitter. You are not broken beyond repair.

You are grieving expectations that were never met. You are mourning moments that were supposed to hold you but left you hollow. You wanted to be seen. To be loved without condition. To be held in your breaking—without needing to explain why you were shattered.

So breathe. Take your time. There is no deadline on healing. And there is no shame in the ache.

Let the Holy Spirit hold what others dropped. Let Her remind you that God sees all of it— the silence, the absence, the betrayal. And God is not indifferent.

God does not call your pain petty. God does not silence your sorrow. God names it. God lifts it. God carries it with you.

And if you are the one who missed the moment— if you were drowning when someone else needed you to stay afloat. There is grace for you, too. Admit it. Own it. Let it teach you how to show up better. But do not let it bury you in shame. God can heal both the hurt and the harm.

So now I speak to both of you— To the one who was forgotten, and to the one who forgot: There is still healing. There is still time. There is still a holy path forward.

And when you are ready, when the tears dry just long enough to speak— tell your story. Not to relive the pain, but to reclaim your power.

Because what they did—or failed to do— What you did — or failed to do— was not the final life.

You are not just surviving. You are sacred. You are still healing— and you are still whole. And oh, sis... you are rising.

Every scar is now a sermon. Every step forward is a victory. Every breath is proof that grace still finds you in the break. So speak your truth— And may the room go silent because the Spirit is bearing witness through you.

And this... this is why Sistaology matters. Because life has a way of wounding us quietly. It teaches us to smile through absence. To pray through pain. To shrink our needs so we do not feel like a burden.

But Sistaology? It teaches us to *breathe out loud.* It is not just a book. It is not just a beautiful idea. It is a movement—a sanctuary—for Black women who are tired of hiding their healing.

This is where the ache is honored. Where the truth is not too much. Where you do not have to explain your tears before they are believed.

Sistaology is what happens when we tell the truth together. And if you are wondering where to find this? *You just did.*

You are holding it in your hands. You are reading the pages of a woman who lived it. And you are now part of this sacred circle.

But we are not stopping here. The community is growing. You can join the Women's Empowerment Network. You can log in to the Women's Empowerment Coffee Break. You can show up as you are—broken, bold, becoming— and find sisters doing the same.

Because here, your story does not get buried. It gets *breathed on*. This is the table. Pull up a chair.

You are not alone anymore. You never were. Sistaology is not just survival. It is resurrection. It is restoration. It is revival.

And it is happening—right now—through us. And still—you rise. Not polished, not perfect, but full of purpose. Because even broken things rise in the Spirit's wind.

Luke 8:54—Jesus says, "Little girl, arise." This is not just resurrection. It is reclamation. Your rise is not rebellion—it is revelation.

From broken pieces, resurrection emerges. You will rise—not in spite of the break, but because of it.

Reflection Prompt:

Think back to a time when the pain did not come from the outside world, but from within your own circle.

Maybe it was a friend, a ministry partner, a sister, or someone you never thought would leave you hanging.

Where were you when you first felt the break?
What were you hoping for in that moment—and what was missing?
How did it change you?
Did it shift how you love? How you trust? How you show up now?
Where did God meet you in the fallout?
Was it in the quiet? In a prayer you whispered through tears?
Did the Spirit show you how to grieve *and* grow?

Write your way through the break.
Let the Holy Spirit reveal the wisdom in the wound.
Let your pen tell the truth—even the messy truth.
Because naming it is the beginning of healing it.

Movement Six: The Rise

When Voice Becomes Power

Finding your rhythm, your authority, your oil.

"Arise, shine, for your light has come, and the glory of the Lord rises upon you." — Isaiah 60:1

I never stopped speaking. But I did shrink. Not because I doubted God's call on my life—but because I wanted to serve without being seen. I wanted to be a team player, not the one holding the mic. I was comfortable working behind the scenes, supporting the mission, making sure things got done. I never needed the spotlight. In fact, I ran from it. I thought if I could just stay in the background, I would still be faithful, still be fruitful—and I was.

But there came a moment when the Spirit would not let me stay hidden. Not because God was trying to elevate me for attention, but because shrinking was starting to silence my authority. I was showing up small in places where God had given me a full-sized word. I was whispering when I should have been declaring. And I realized that hiding was not humility—it was fear dressed up as obedience.

God never asked me to disappear in order to serve. The more I started walking in my assignment, the more I realized that voice is not about visibility—it is about *vessel*. It is not

85

about being the loudest. It is about being *led*. When God gives you a word, it is not for you to keep tucked away. It is meant to speak life into dry places. It is meant to stir what has been stuck. It is meant to confront, comfort, and call people—including yourself—back to the Spirit.

I started to notice that when I used my voice—whether in prayer, teaching, preaching, writing, or just telling the truth in conversation—something shifted. Not always around me, but *in* me. I felt more grounded. I felt more bold. I felt more whole. And that is when I began to understand: *voice is power*.

Not the kind of power the world talks about. This power is different. It does not control—it carries. It carries truth. It carries wisdom. It carries oil. And every time I released what God put in me, the Spirit met me in the release.

I speak. Not to impress, but to be in alignment.

I speak because shrinking is no longer an option.

I speak because I have something to say—and not because I need it to be heard by everyone, but because I need to be faithful to the One who gave it to me.

And you—your voice has power too. Even if it shakes. Even if it comes out quietly. Even if it feels unfinished. If it is real, if it is rooted, if it is Spirit-led, then it is enough. So speak, and trust the oil on your voice.

The Honesty of Rise

Let me be honest. I have not fully arrived at *the rise*. Some days I still feel stuck. One moment I am walking in clarity, the next I am sitting in confusion wondering if I missed the turn. I go back and forth between movements because I still need the Spirit to show up in different ways. That is the truth. And if you are anything like me, you know what it means to rise, fall, and rise again. Do not let anybody make you think that once you rise, you are done. The rising is continuous. It is layered. And it is sacred.

For me, rising has looked like saying yes to God when everything in me wanted to say no. It has looked like wiping my tears, gathering my thoughts, and following the Spirit's instructions even when my emotions were louder than my faith. Obedience has always been the push that lifts me— every time I get off track, the Spirit gives me that subtle nudge to come back. And when I respond, I feel the ground beneath me shift.

There was a time when I was not trying to be seen, but I *was* trying to be believed. I wanted people to understand I was called by God. I tried to explain it, defend it, prove it. Some people supported me, others thought I was doing too much or doing it all wrong. It took time for me to realize that the rhythm God gave me was not for public approval. It was not a sound they needed to hear—it was a flow I had to learn to trust. And when I stopped explaining and just walked in it, I discovered that God's rhythm was the best song I would ever dance to.

I did not trust that rhythm all at once. It took storms. It took going through and coming out. Every time the darkness lifted and a crack of sunlight hit my path, I found myself moving with more confidence. Not because everything was perfect, but because I had survived another wave. That is when I started trusting the flow. Not the hustle. Not the performance. But the holy rhythm of the Spirit walking with me.

And yes—I remember the first time I felt authority rising in me. I was a social worker leading education groups for a 28-day residential rehab center. Every day, I had to stand in front of people and speak. That terrified me. Public speaking was never my thing. I used to stumble over my words, afraid someone would laugh at me or call me out for not making sense. But I did it. Day after day. And somewhere along the way, the stumbles turned into steady steps. The fear turned into fuel. I knew then that God had given me a voice not to impress but to impact.

Lived experience taught me more than any title ever could. A title might get you a seat at the table, but it is your scars that teach you how to serve. People may not always respect your role, but they can feel the oil when it flows from a place of truth. They can see the power in your survival. And even if they do not, God still draws people through your overcoming.

My oil? It formed in the press. It formed in my upbringing—watching my parents push through hardship with faith and grit. It formed in the way I kept going after being teased in school, after losing confidence, after carrying the weight of disappointment. It showed up in the drive that would not let me quit, even when the odds were stacked high. I did not always recognize it as oil. But now I see clearly—the anointing was there in every moment I chose to keep going. It was the Holy Spirit carrying me forward.

I began to embrace my story the day I started seeing my scars as sacred. The stretch marks. The c-section scar. They reminded me that I had become a mother. That something painful gave way to something beautiful. Life left marks on me—but I wear them like proof. They remind me that I did not break down, I broke *through*. The bruises, the burnt bits—they are not my shame. They are my testimony.

There was a season when I stayed home for six years, taking care of my family. I had just earned my Bachelor's degree. I was newly married. I got pregnant—and then I lost the baby. That miscarriage broke something in me. And yet, in the silence of that grief, I chose to stay. To nurture. To mother. To serve my household when the world could not see it as a rise. But it *was* a rise. It may have looked like comfort to others, but to me, it was obedience. It was healing. It was holy.

Eventually, I rose above the expectations. Above what others thought I should be doing. I stopped trying to meet their timeline and followed God's instruction instead. That was a rise no one could define but God.

I know the world sees rising as power, fame, money, visibility. But that is not the rise I know. Spirit-led rising is quiet sometimes. But it is disruptive. It is bold. It does not chase influence. It walks in authority. It irritates those who cannot recognize the Spirit because it carries justice, truth, and holiness. It is not loud for attention. It is sacred because it comes from God.

So if you are rising slowly, if you are unsure, if you feel like you are in between movements—hear me. That is still the rise. The rhythm will come. The authority is growing. And the oil is already there. Keep going.

The Rhythm Is Mine

I started listening for rhythm. Not the rhythm of the crowd or the pattern of what seemed successful. But the rhythm of the Spirit. It came in moments of surrender. In the quiet decisions no one saw. In the times I let go of who I was trying to be and trusted who God was shaping me to become. My rhythm did not match the timelines I saw around me. It did not match the expectations people placed on me. But it was real. And it was mine.

I had to learn how to walk with my voice, not just use it. I had to trust that the same Spirit who gave me the power to speak would give me the strength to rise. Not just once. But again and again. Because the rise is not a single moment—it is a movement. A holy rhythm that builds as you keep stepping in obedience, keep dancing to the beat only you can hear.

Stop trying to get to where others think you ought to be. That kind of pressure will water you down. You will start shifting your shape to fit their expectations, and the next thing you know, you are performing instead of living. Let me tell you—your authenticity is what people need. Not the version of you who is rushing to meet someone else's deadline, but the one who is growing with God in real time.

Social media has a way of making people feel like they are behind. You scroll and see engagements, career moves, speaking invitations, matching outfits, and staged joy. Most of the time, people only post the best moments and hide the ones that took them through hell. What they do not show is the breakdown before the breakthrough. You do not see the hospital visits, the quiet tears, the arguments, the nights they wanted to quit. You just see the shine. And you start questioning your steps because you assume their highlight reel is the full story. Let me remind you: we are all walking different paths. And we will all arrive in different ways.

I had to stop looking over my shoulder. I had to stop mimicking someone else's move when God was teaching me a new rhythm. My rhythm in motherhood looked like rocking babies at 2 AM, and reflecting over my life in between wiping tears. My rhythm in ministry looked like learning to be faithful behind the scenes—when no one was clapping, and the only one who saw me was God. My rhythm in career looked like walking away from job titles and trusting the Spirit's instructions, even when they made no sense to others.

Trusting your rhythm means trusting your revelation. What has God whispered to *you*? What has the Spirit shown you in private that no one else could understand? You do not need to rush. You do not need to copy. You do not need to over explain. What you need to do is tune in. Feel the nudge. Listen for the shift. Honor your divine pace.

I Walk Different Now

When you know who you are, you walk differently. There is a posture, a presence, a peace. You are not waiting on someone else to say you are enough. God already did. So you walk forward, even if there are obstacles in front of you and confusion all around you. You keep pushing because God gave you the strength for the journey. People who carry the Spirit can feel it. People who do not? You will confuse them, and that is fine. Let them wonder.

When I rose in authority, I had to change my boundaries. I stopped accepting limitations that others tried to place on me. I moved when they said stop. I obeyed the Spirit when they said wait. Even my quiet decisions started sounding like threats to people who could no longer control me. I learned that just being who God called me to be was enough to make some people uncomfortable—and that was not my problem to fix.

I remember having to stand in my truth while my voice trembled. I was unsure. I was scared. But I stood anyway. I told the truth about my calling, even when others questioned it. I showed up when I wanted to shrink. And one day, someone told me, "You have faith that I have never seen before. Like you know who you are in God." I had not even realized it. I was still healing. Still growing. Still becoming. But the Spirit was visible, even in my uncertainty.

Authority is not loud. It is steady. It is Spirit-rooted. It moves with conviction, not convenience. When you carry that kind of authority, you do not have to announce it. It announces you.

There's Oil on That

There are places in my life that once made me feel ashamed. Situations that confused me. Decisions that I regretted. But when I look back now, I can say with confidence—there was oil on that. I did not always see it. Sometimes it looked too messy to hold. Too painful to touch. I just knew something was different, but I could not explain it. Now I know—it was the press.

I have made some hard decisions. I have walked through heartbreak. I have faced delays that made me question whether God had forgotten about me. But every single time, I came out wiser. Stronger. More Spirit-aware. I began to understand that the pressing was not punishment. It was preparation. God was producing something in me that changed what was required to handle the weight.

My scars tell that story. The physical ones and the invisible ones. When I trace them, I do not see failure anymore. I see fruit. I see favor. I see the fingerprints of God shaping me into the woman I was always becoming. The healing after the miscarriages and stillbirth. The pain of starting over. All of it—anointed.

So, let me ask you: what do you see in your scars? Can you look past the wound and see the witness? Can you name what God produced through what you endured? Do not just remember the pain. Remember the oil. Remember the *blessing* it produced. You did not come through that for nothing.

There is oil on that. Your rise was never meant to end with you. What caught fire in your life is meant to catch flame in someone else's.

Acts 2:3–4—the Spirit fell as tongues of fire. The early church was born not in silence but in power. Your fire is not to warm you alone—it is to awaken nations.

Your rise is not the finale. It is the spark. What God lit in you will ignite the world.

Reflection Prompt

So, speak, and trust the oil on your voice. And as you speak, pay attention: **Where might you still be shrinking? Where is God inviting you to open your mouth fully, without apology?**

The rhythm is beginning to move. Let it carry you. As you walk, listen for the places where you have tried to match a pace that was never yours.

Whose timeline have you been measuring yourself against?

Release it now, and rest in the rhythm God set for you. And as you stand taller, ask yourself: **Where have I hesitated to walk in full authority? What boundaries is God strengthening so that I no longer shrink for anyone's comfort?**

Look again at the places you once tried to hide. **Can you see the oil forming in those very places?** Let the Spirit show you how nothing was wasted. This is your rise. Quiet, steady, holy. You are not late. You are not behind. You are becoming. Stay with God's pace, and trust that every step is part of your rise.

Movement Seven: The Fire

When others catch the flame.

Legacy. Multiplication. Anointing. The bridge.

"I will pour out my Spirit on all people. Your sons and daughters will prophesy." — Joel 2:28

The fire was never just for me. And it is not just for you either. When the Spirit begins to burn within us, it is never for the purpose of staying small. This flame we carry is not decorative—it is *declarative*. It declares that God is not done with us. It declares that every movement we have survived has prepared us to become vessels of something bigger. This fire is a testimony—and it is catching.

I knew the flame was spreading when I became honest that I had not fully risen. And still—my becoming was blessing others. Not my arrival. My *honesty*. When I let people see the unpolished places, the scars, the sacrifices—it stirred something in them. Because realness makes room for restoration. And if I can still be becoming and still keep going—so can they.

Some people told me directly that my story lit a fire in them. Others never said a word. But I learned a long time ago: just because they do not tell you, does not mean the Spirit is not using you. Our job is not to track the fire. It is to *tend it.* To protect the oil. To pour it faithfully and let God multiply it.

My story has multiplied because I chose to be honest. I admitted when my faith felt like it was hanging by a thread. I reached for the seed—the literal mustard seed—and carried it in my purse like a silent prayer. "God, I am holding on to this as proof that I still believe... barely. But please, if You are blessing in this season—do not do it without me." That was not performance. That was pain. That was desperation. But it was also *fire*. Because even crushed hope can burn.

Legacy now means something different to me. It is not about finishing everything I start. It is about leaving something for someone else to build on. It is being willing to walk away with the puzzle unfinished—because you trust the Spirit to place the final piece.

That lesson hit me during a workshop at Princeton Theological Seminary with Dr. Lakisha Lockhart-Rusch. We were asked to complete a puzzle, but it was designed to be incomplete. No picture on the box. Pieces missing. Team members with restricted roles. No one could do it alone. When time ran out and it was still undone, something in me felt like I had failed. But then I realized—the goal was never to finish it. The goal was to trust the process and follow the instructions. That is legacy. That is fire. It is obedience without obsession over the outcome.

God has used even my small yeses to build bridges. A willingness to work with people even when we disagree. Choosing understanding instead of ego. Sharing wisdom instead of hoarding it. Every time I pour, the Spirit pours back into me. Even when I have emptied myself dry, somehow—God finds a way to refill me.

This fire does not depend on my strength. It depends on the breath of God. And I have watched this fire spread in places I never expected. I think of my children. My oldest son's quiet determination. My daughter's persistence that will not let up. My youngest son's boldness and joy. They are walking on ground I broke through prayer, tears, and late-night surrender. They are already standing on my ceiling. And that is legacy.

This book, this calling—it has felt heavy. Like too much. Like the anointing is too thick for me to carry on my own. And that is exactly how I know it is God. Because I could not do this without the Holy Spirit. On the days I had no words, people checked in. Prayed for me. Sat with me in silence. I made it this far on the prayers of others and the breath of God. Period.

There were days when I thought the fire would go out. Disappointment tried to choke it. Fatigue tried to drown it. But then I remembered: fire does not need applause. It just needs air. And as long as I have breath in my body, the Spirit will keep breathing on my flame.

Not everyone will celebrate your fire. Some will keep their distance. Some will feel a way about your favor. I have learned not to take it personally. I know what it is to watch someone rise while you are still trying to survive. It is not always jealousy—it is pain. And that pain deserves grace. Because if you have ever burned through a season of loss or delay, you know how hard it is to watch someone else shine. Maturity says, "I see you. I still bless you. And I will wait for my turn without bitterness."

Because fire does not compete. It *connects*.

And when the Spirit is in it, it will multiply.

To the one reading this: you are not just holding my words. You are holding the witness of what God has done. And you are holding a flame of your own. You have fire too. It may be flickering. It may be hiding under grief. It may be dim from the winds of life. But it is still there.

Let this be your reminder: the flame you carry will outlive you. It will pass through your children, your students, your friends, your community, your story. If you let it. If you pour it. If you believe again.

So who will carry the oil after us? All who are willing. All who are watching. All who are asking the Spirit to move fresh and new. And when the fire marks you, it leaves a stain. Oil that will not wash out. Glory that lingers.

Let the next generation inherit the anointing that breaks every yoke. Let them see Black women's stories and not try to rewrite them, but *feel* them. Sit with them. Stand beside them. Do not cross the bridge just to manage us. Cross the bridge to *march with us*.

Protect the flame. Do not put it out. Because this movement will not die. This Spirit will not fade. This fire will not burn out. Sistaology is more than Black women's stories. It is a flame. It is a legacy. And it is yours, too.

So light the match. Breathe in the flame. Carry the oil. And let it burn.

Look at You, Oil-Bearer

You are next. You are chosen. Now go. You, daughter of God. Yes—you. The one who almost put the flame down. The one who questioned if your yes still mattered. The one who carries so much oil but has been too exhausted to pour.

Let me tell you what the Spirit is whispering in your direction: **Look at you, oil-bearer.** Still standing. Still believing. Still showing up to the fire even when your hands have been shaking. You thought it skipped over you? You thought the anointing was for someone else?

No, beloved. **The flame is in you. It always was.** You have survived enough. You have wept enough. You have waited long enough. And now, the Spirit is saying: *Rise. With the fire still in your bones.*

Your breath is proof that God is not done. Your story still has smoke rising from it. The very places that nearly broke you have been soaked in oil. And the time has come for you to carry the flame forward.

You are not a flicker. You are not forgotten. You are not too late. You are not too much. **You are fire. You are oil. You are the one the Spirit chose to burn through.**

So light the match again. Let your scars speak in rooms that once silenced you. Let your testimony raise up daughters who thought survival was the end. Let your yes call down glory. Let your worship make room for the next woman's healing. Let your words unlock someone else's wind.

You are not just reading this. You are being reignited by it. So stand up, sis. Straighten your crown. Stretch your arms toward heaven. And feel the wind of the Spirit blowing fresh fire into your story. **You are next. You are chosen. Now go.**

To the Flame Carriers

This movement will not end with a whisper. It will not fade into a footnote. It will not be reduced to emotion or memory. The fire of *Sistaology* was never meant to stay confined to the page. It was meant to *pass*—from life to life, hand to hand, flame to flame.

And now, beloved—

It is in your hands.

You are a flame carrier.

Not because everything in your life is figured out. Not because your story is polished or perfect. But because God has trusted you with fire.

You were not left behind. You were not overlooked. You were preserved. The matches you have been afraid to strike? Strike them. The dreams you buried to survive? Dig them up. The oil you doubted was still flowing? Touch it. Feel it. Pour it.

There are people waiting on your rise. There are rooms waiting on your sound. There are generations waiting on

your faith. There are daughters, sisters, and strangers—
waiting for your fire to testify.

You do not need a pulpit to be powerful. You do not need
a title to be trusted. You do not need permission to become.

You just need to say yes. To rise. To burn. To *become*
what the Spirit is igniting in you.

Let your steps be embers. Let your breath be wind.
Let your presence be proof. Let your life be the flame that
tells the next woman: "You can burn too."

This is your commission. This is your call. This is your
fire. **Carry it well. Carry it boldly. Carry it together.**

And never forget: You are not just in the fire. You are
made of it.

The Altar

When the Flame Finds You

This is not the end of the book— It is the beginning of your next "yes." The altar is not behind you. It is wherever you are willing to burn.

Altar Call: If You're Ready to Burn

If you do not know Jesus as you personal Savior, today I offer you Jesus. If you are reading this and feel the pull in your chest—the trembling in your belly—that is not coincidence. That is the Holy Spirit saying, **"This is your moment. Come alive again."**

If you have been dimming your fire for too long— If you have been waiting for someone else to give you permission—If you have been pouring and wondering if anything will ever pour back into you—Then this call is for *you.*

This is your altar. Wherever you are—on the floor of your living room, in the corner of your car, with a journal open on your lap—**Make that place holy.**

Lay down what you have been carrying. And say out loud if you can: "God, I give You my life. I give You my flame. I give You my yes. I give You my fear, my fatigue, my doubt.

I give You my story—the bruised, the bold, and the breaking parts.

Breathe on me again. Light me up. And use me for Your glory. I will carry the fire. I will not shrink back. I am Yours."

Now breathe. Sit still. Let the Spirit wash over you.

And know— You are no longer standing alone. You are standing in the fire. And you are surrounded by a cloud of witnesses. By sisters who burn. By generations of oil-bearers who never stopped pouring. By the presence of God that never left your side.

This is your altar. This is your rising. This is your flame.

Let it burn.

Closing Prayer: Come, Holy Spirit

Breathe on every daughter holding this page.

Breathe on the one who has grown tired in the waiting.

Breathe on the one who has questioned if she still carries anything worth igniting.

Let Your flame fall fresh again. Reignite what has grown dim. Uncover what shame tried to bury. Wake up the gifts that disappointment tried to silence. Let the wind of Your Spirit swirl through her soul until she remembers—*she was always flame, always oil, always chosen.*

Fan the fire, God. Let the broken places become burning places. Let the ashes become altars. Let her body remember what it feels like to be filled. Let her voice rise again with power.

Wherever she is reading—make it holy ground. Wherever she is grieving—let glory find her. Wherever she is doubting—let the fire speak louder.

We do not want to just feel better. We want to be *consumed*. We want to be *used*. We want to *burn*—for You and because of You.

So light her up, Lord. Until her words testify. Until her hands heal. Until her obedience unlocks generations. Until every room she walks in is marked by smoke.

Come, Holy Spirit. Fall fresh. Fall holy. Fall now.

Amen.

Scripture Index

Below is a listing of the Scripture references that have anchored and breathed through each movement of this book:

Movement One: The Stretch – Luke 1:45

Movement Two: The Silence – Psalm 46:10

Movement Three: The Breath – Genesis 2:7

Movement Four: The Story – Revelation 12:11

Movement Five: The Break – Psalm 147:3

Movement Six: The Rise – Isaiah 60:1

Movement Seven: The Fire – Joel 2:28

Anointing Confessions and Reflection Notes

Use the following pages to record your prayers, your stretches, your yes, and your moments of burning. This is your altar. Speak freely. Write prophetically. Anoint boldly.

_____

_____

_____

_____

_____

_____

_____

_____

_____

_____

_____

_____

_____

_____

_____

_____